LEONARD BERNSTEIN
10 SELECTIONS FROM "CANDIDE"

Arranged by Charlie Harmon

ISBN 978-1-4234-5835-7

LEONARD
BERNSTEIN
Music Publishing
Company LLC

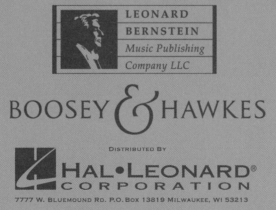

BOOSEY & HAWKES

DISTRIBUTED BY

HAL•LEONARD®
CORPORATION
7777 W. BLUEMOUND RD. P.O. BOX 13819 MILWAUKEE, WI 53213

www.boosey.com
www.halleonard.com

CONTENTS

Overture to "Candide" 2

The Best of All Possible Worlds 26

Oh, Happy We 36

Candide Continues His Travels / It Must Be Me 40

Paris Waltz 42

I Am Easily Assimilated 52

Ballad of Eldorado 62

Bon Voyage (Hornpipe) 68

We Are Women (Polka) 78

Make Our Garden Grow 88

10 SELECTIONS FROM "CANDIDE"

Overture to "Candide"

Allegro molto con brio (♩ = 132)

Leonard Bernstein
Arranged by C Harmon

Secondo

10 SELECTIONS FROM "CANDIDE"
Overture to "Candide"

Allegro molto con brio (♩ = 132)

Leonard Bernstein
Arranged by C Harmon

Primo

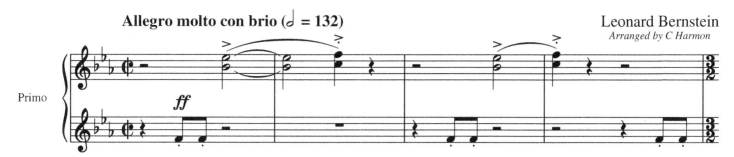

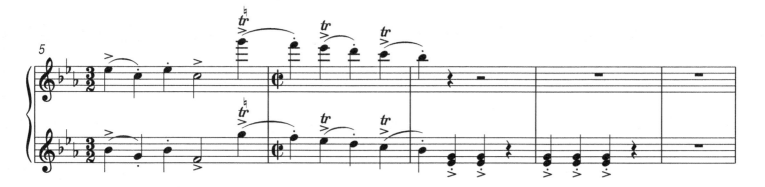

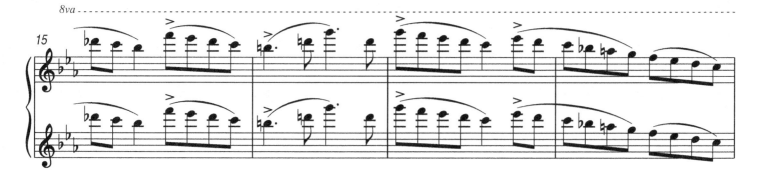

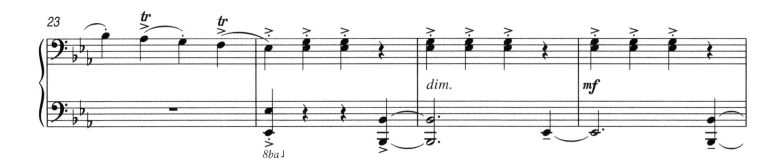

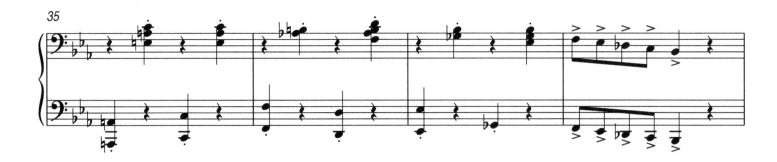

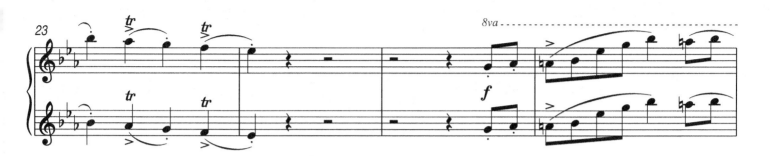

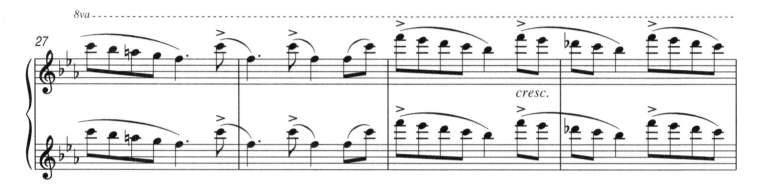

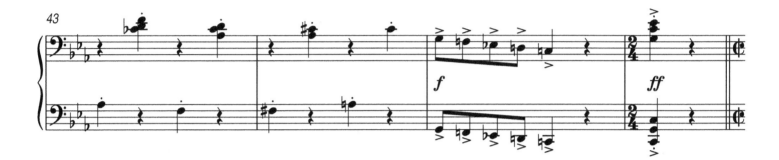

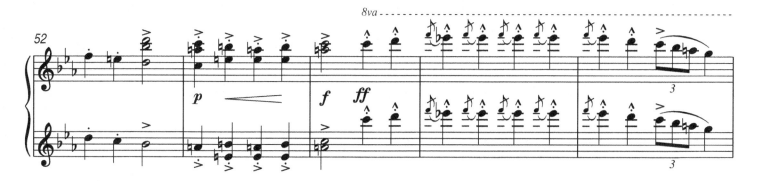

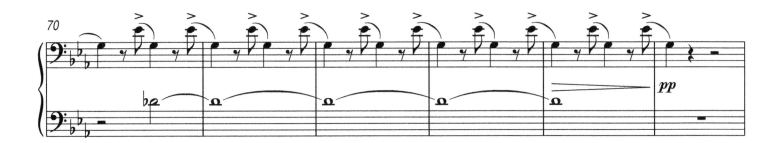

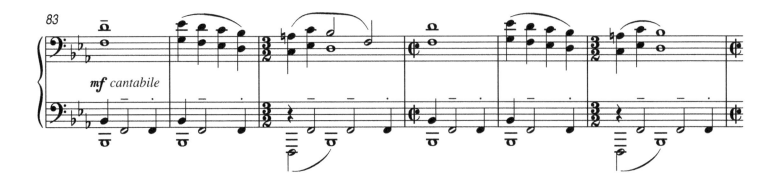

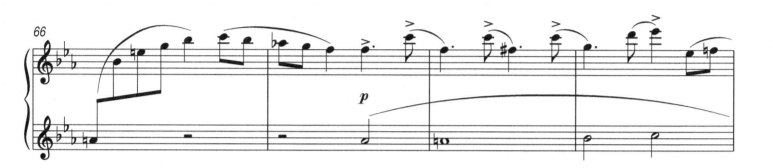

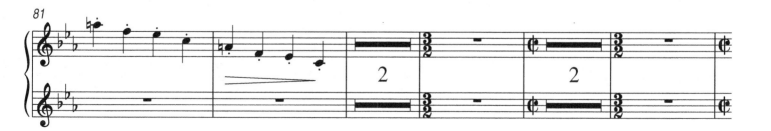

Secondo

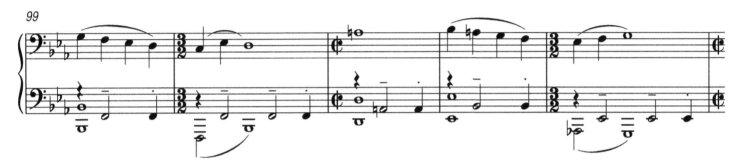

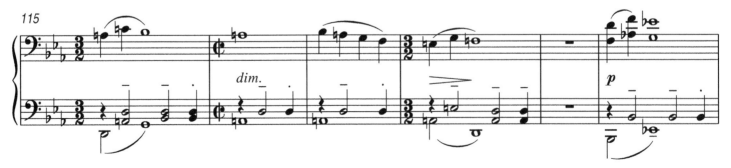

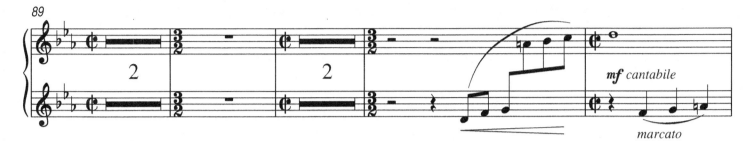

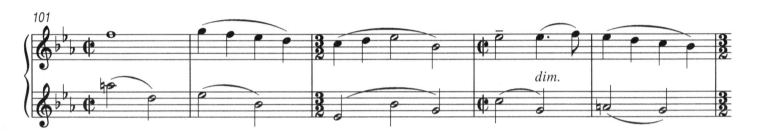

Secondo

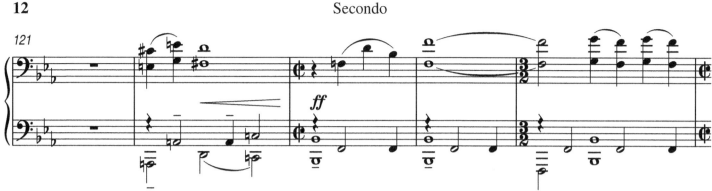

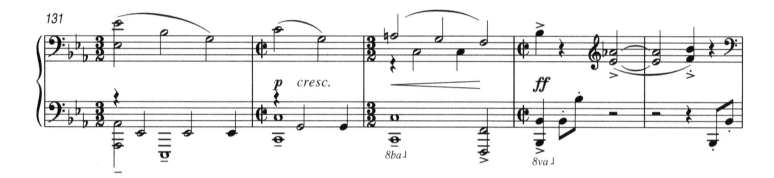

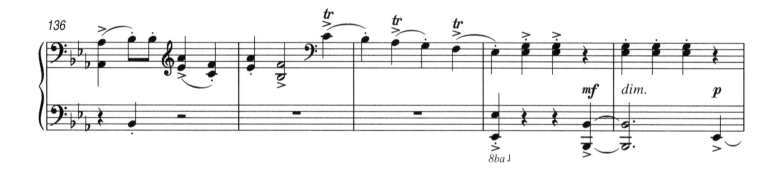

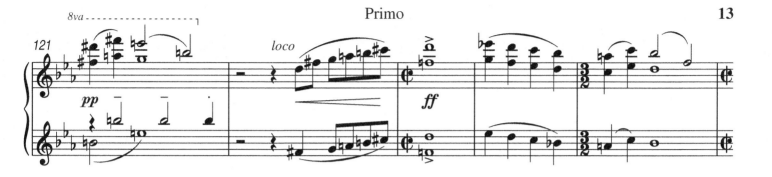

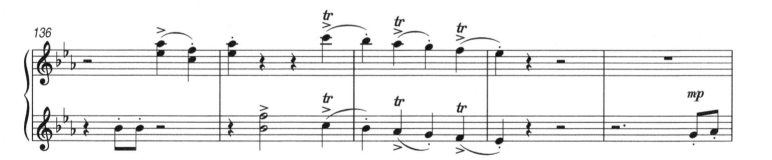

Secondo

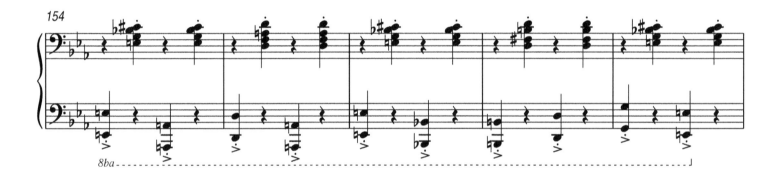

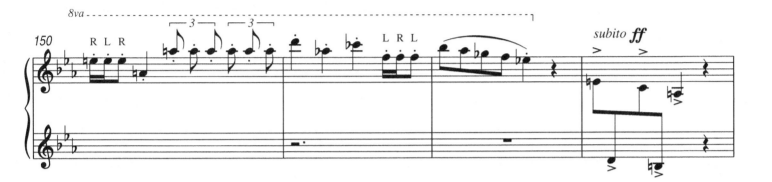

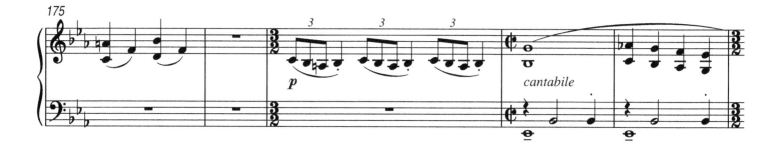

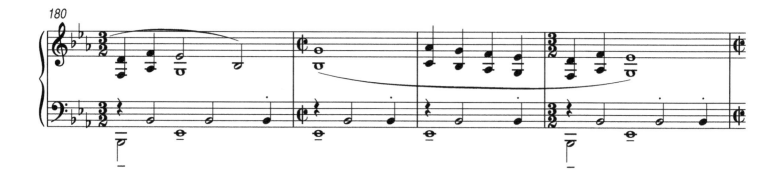

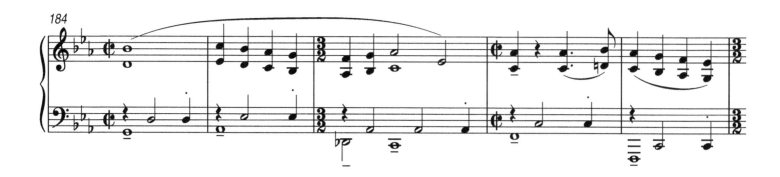

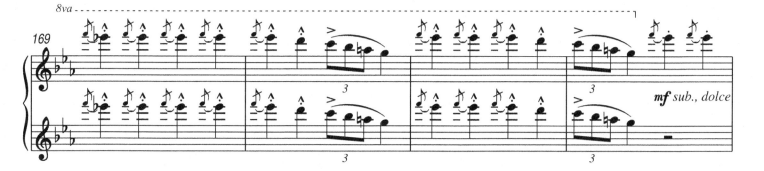

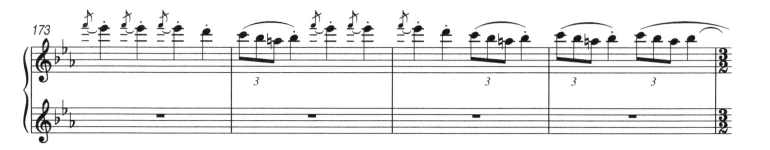

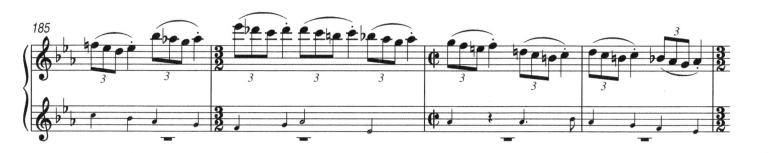

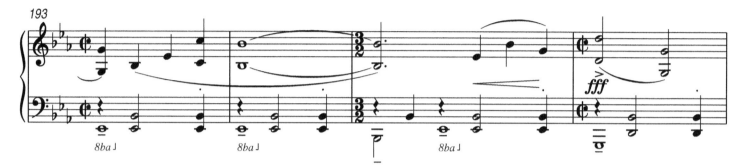

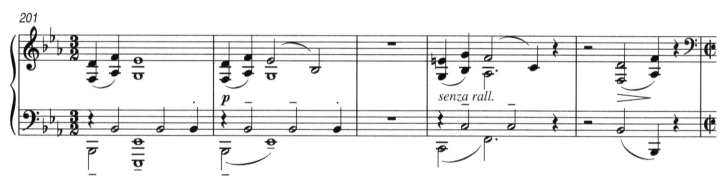

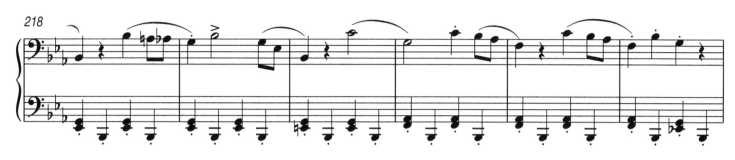

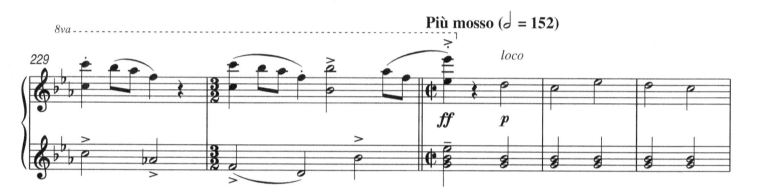

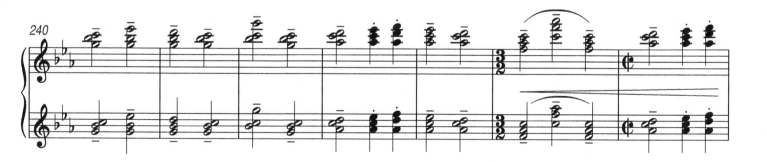

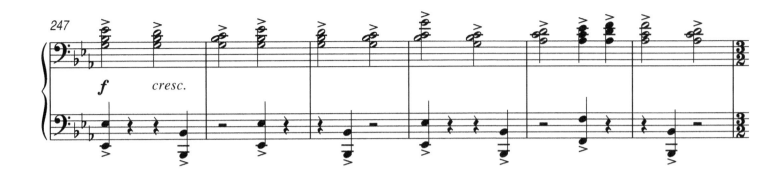

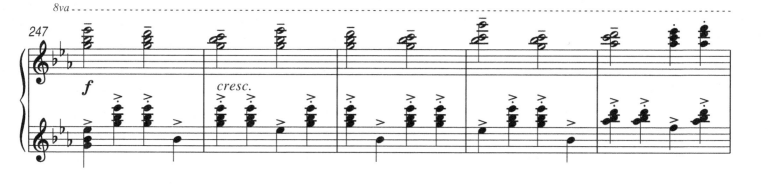

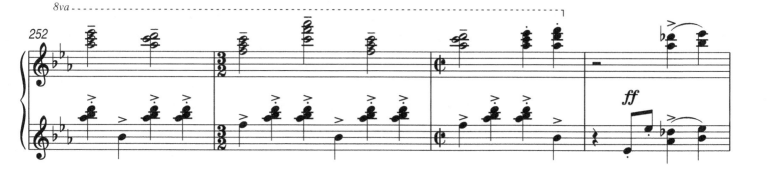

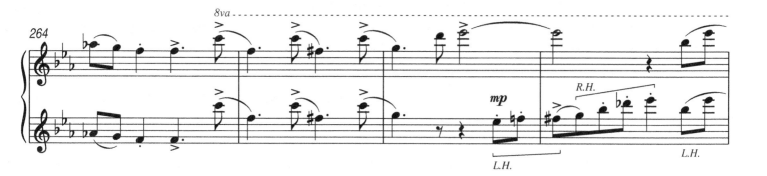

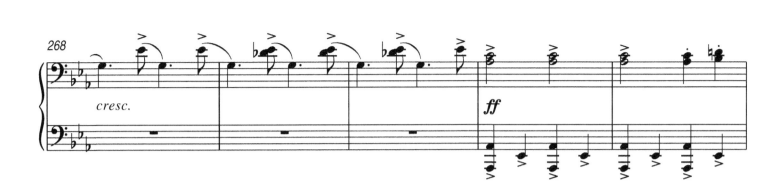

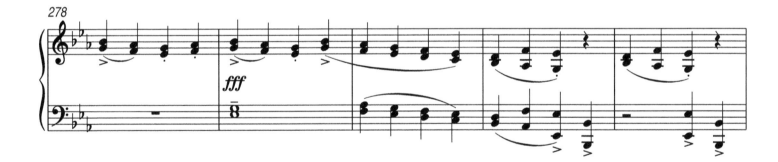

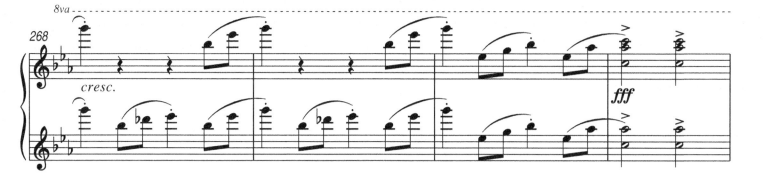

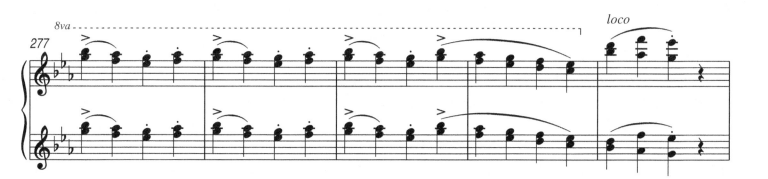

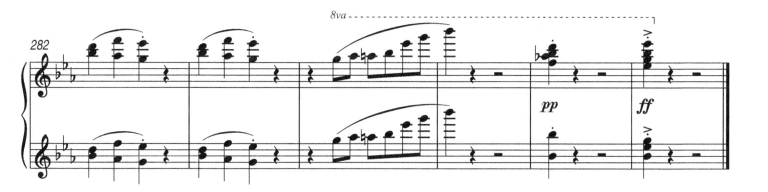

The Best of All Possible Worlds

Allegretto (bright and fast)

Leonard Bernstein
Arranged by C Harmon

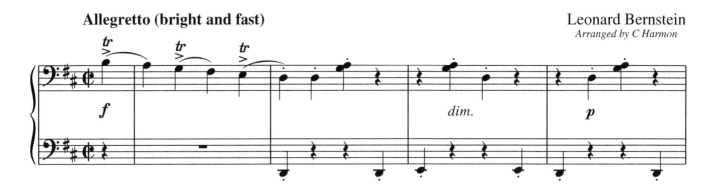

The Best of All Possible Worlds

Allegretto (bright and fast)

Leonard Bernstein
Arranged by C Harmon

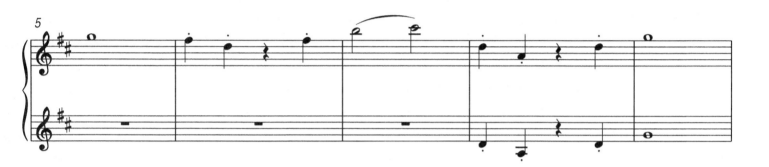

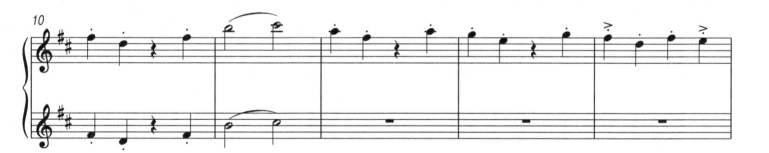

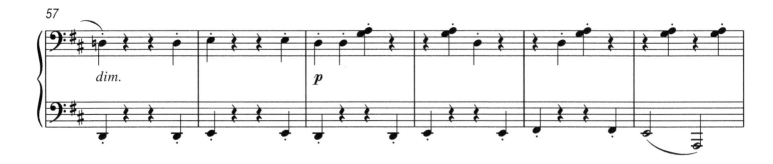

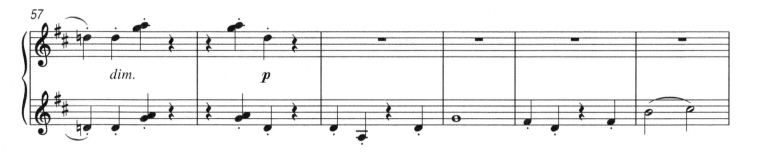

Secondo

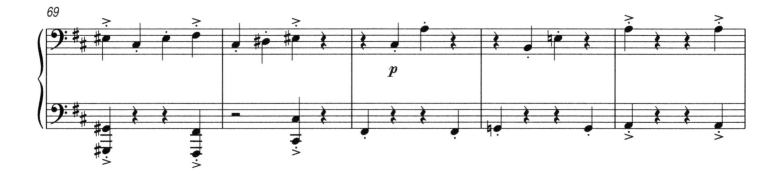

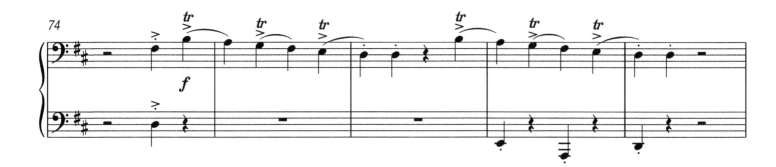

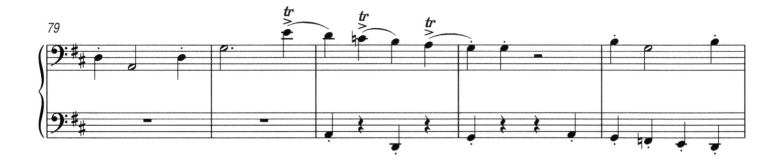

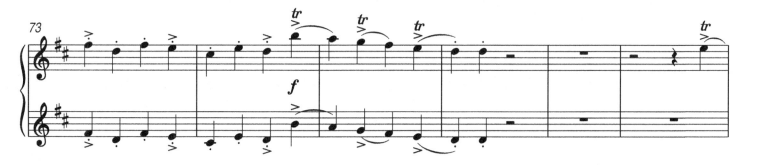

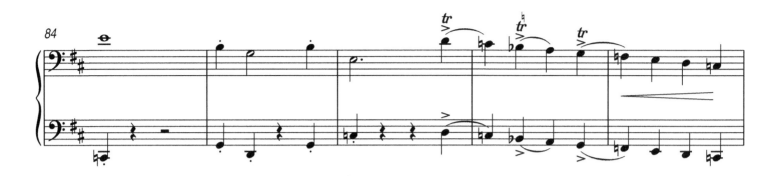

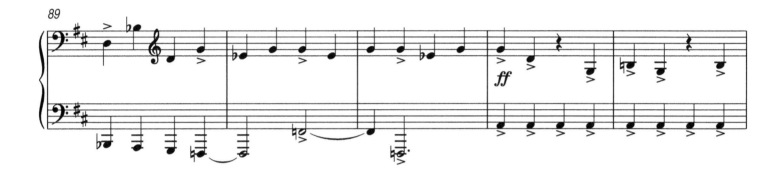

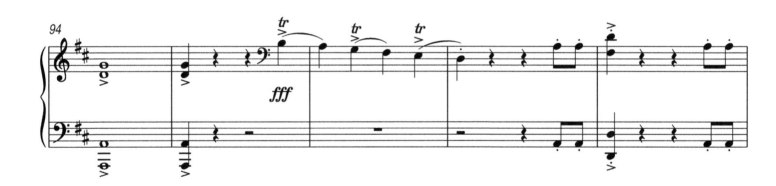

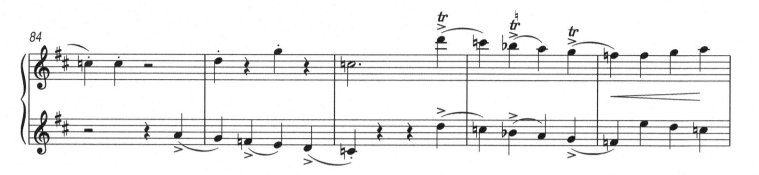

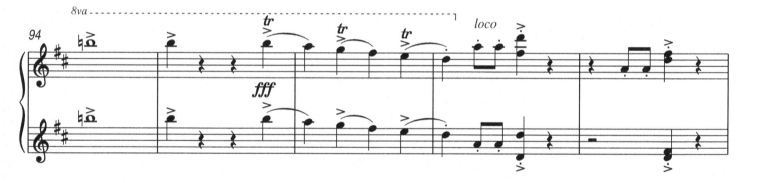

Oh, Happy We

Leonard Bernstein
Arranged by C Harmon

Allegretto con anima

Oh, Happy We

Allegretto con anima

Leonard Bernstein
Arranged by C Harmon

Candide Continues His Travels / It Must Be Me

Leonard Bernstein
Arranged by C Harmon

Andante

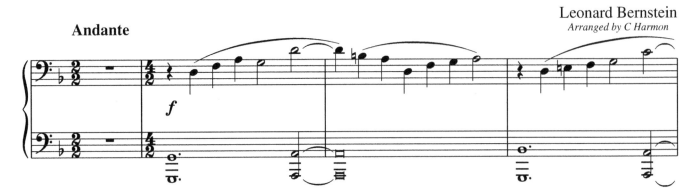

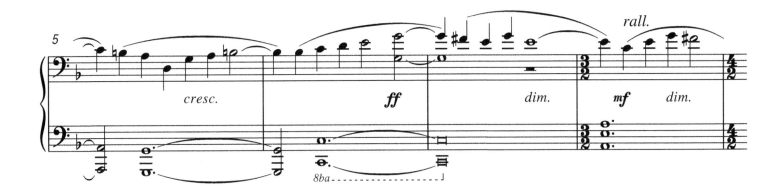

Slow and free, like a folk song

Candide Continues His Travels / It Must Be Me

Leonard Bernstein
Arranged by C Harmon

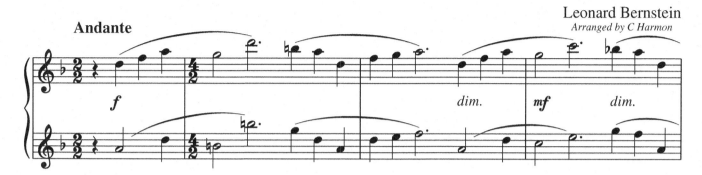

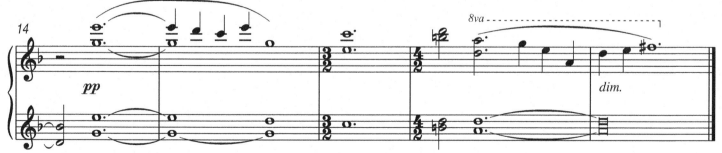

Paris Waltz

Leonard Bernstein
Arranged by C Harmon

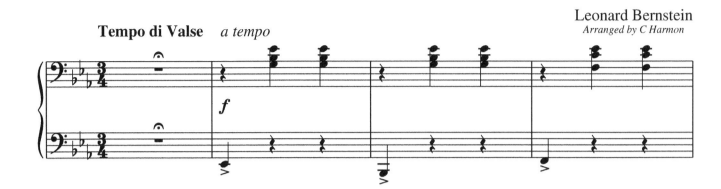

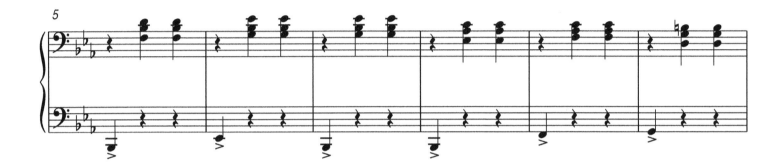

Paris Waltz

Leonard Bernstein
Arranged by C Harmon

Secondo

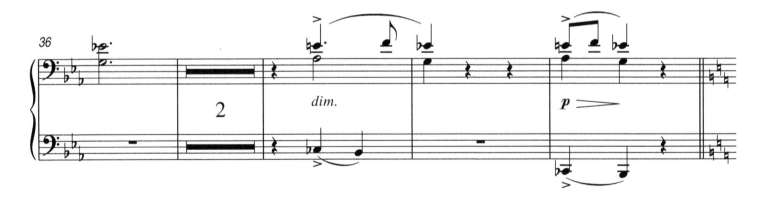

poco dim.

dim.

p >

p

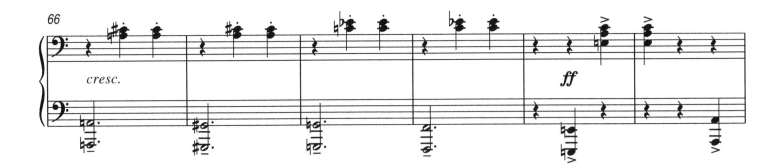

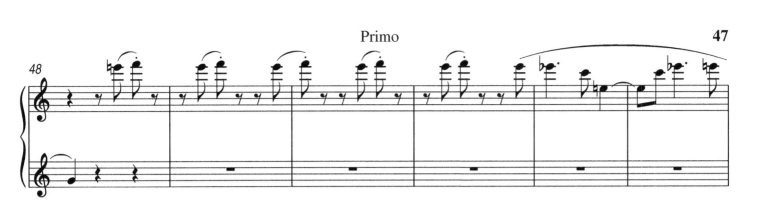

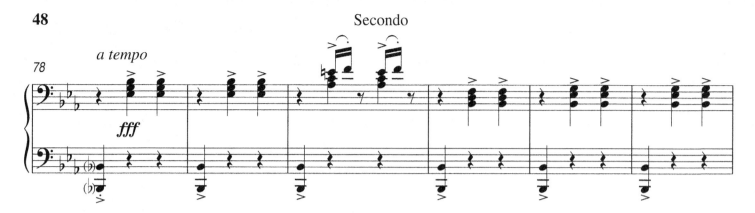

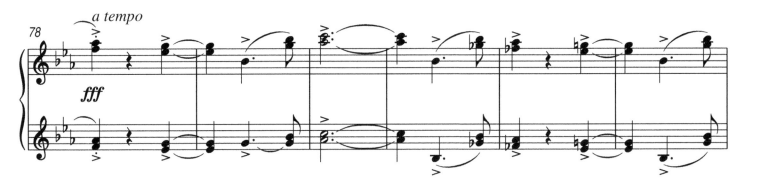

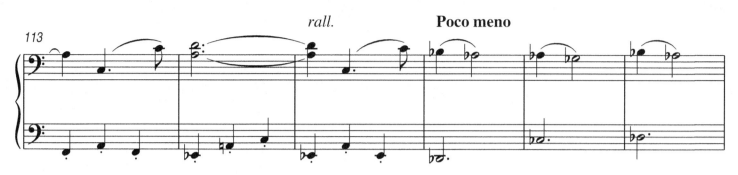

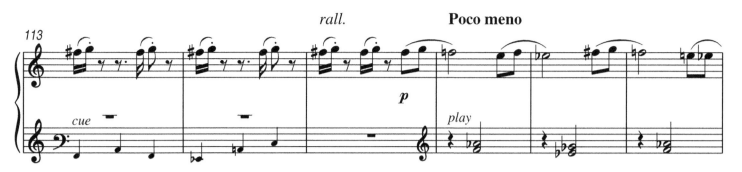

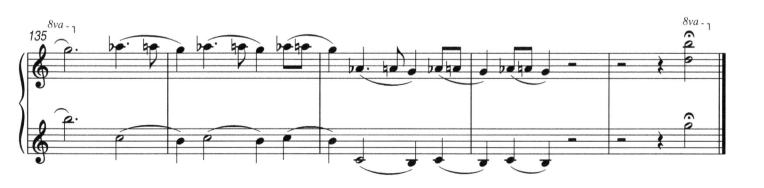

I Am Easily Assimilated

Moderato

Leonard Bernstein
Arranged by C Harmon

I Am Easily Assimilated

Leonard Bernstein
Arranged by C Harmon

Secondo

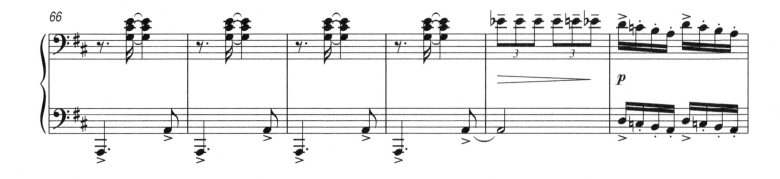

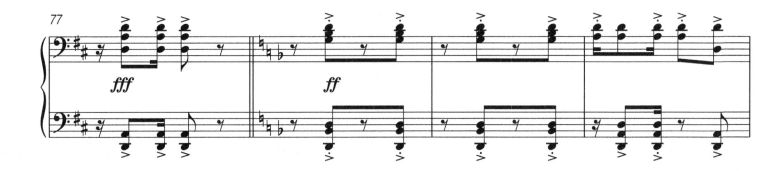

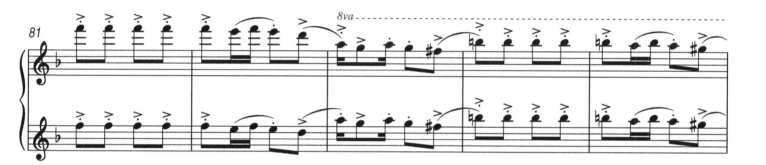

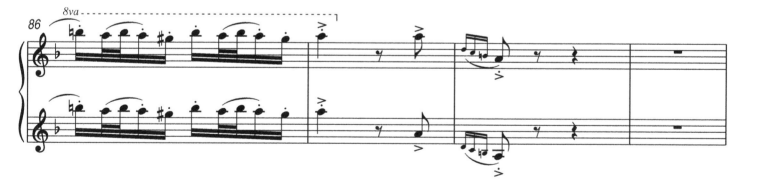

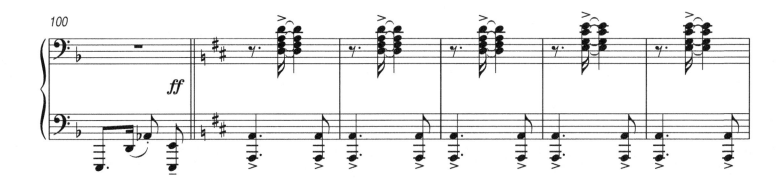

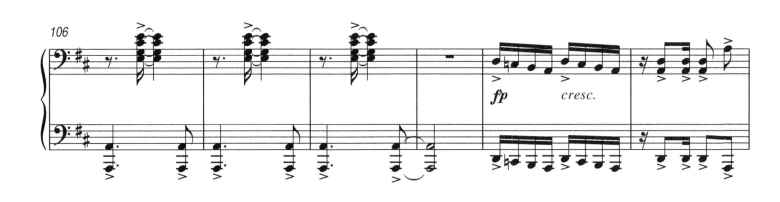

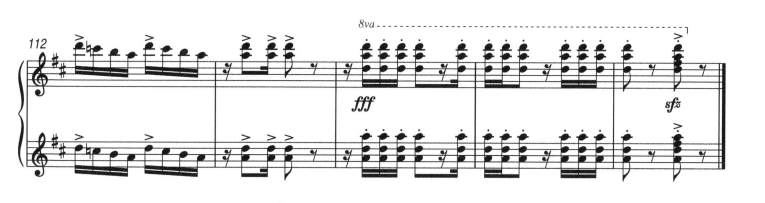

Secondo

Ballad of Eldorado

Leonard Bernstein
Arranged by C Harmon

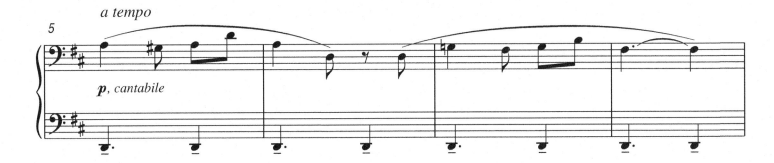

Ballad of Eldorado

Leonard Bernstein
Arranged by C Harmon

Allegretto

a tempo

23

28

33
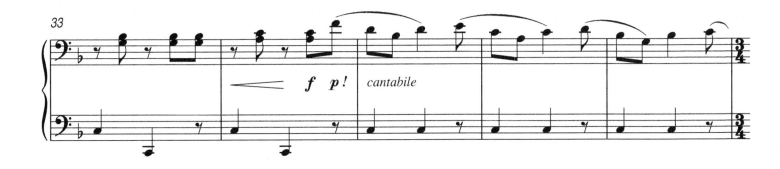

38

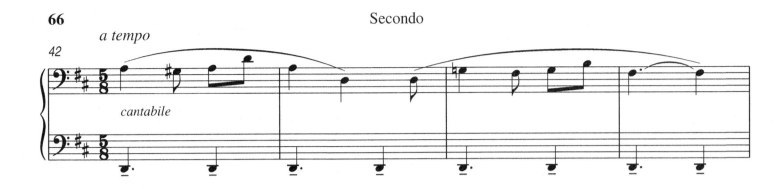

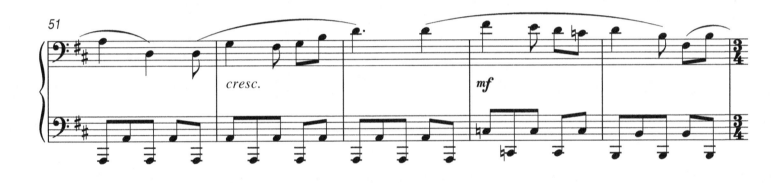

Bon Voyage
(Hornpipe)

Leonard Bernstein
Arranged by C Harmon

Allegretto vivace

Bon Voyage
(Hornpipe)

Leonard Bernstein
Arranged by C Harmon

Allegretto vivace

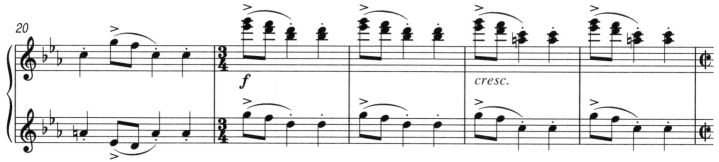

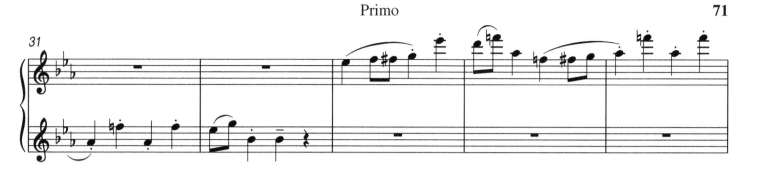

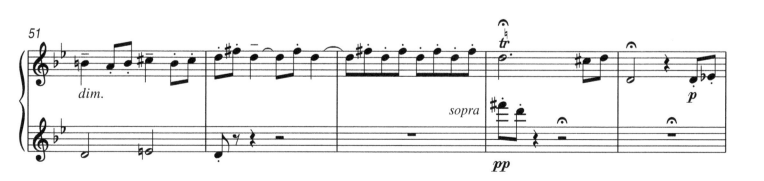

Secondo

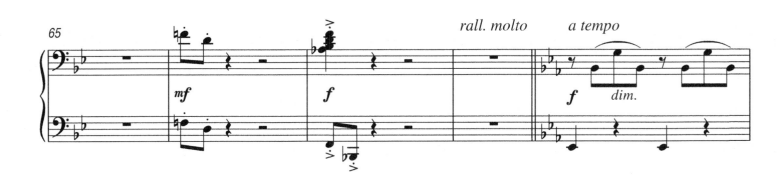

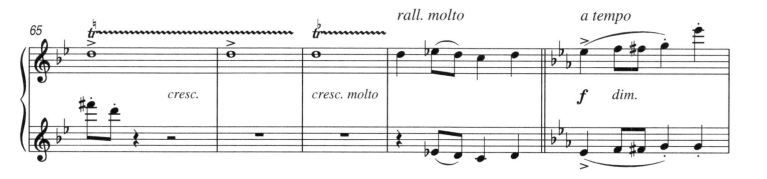

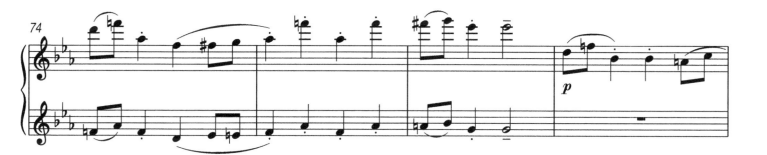

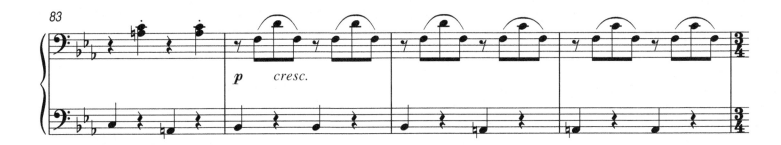

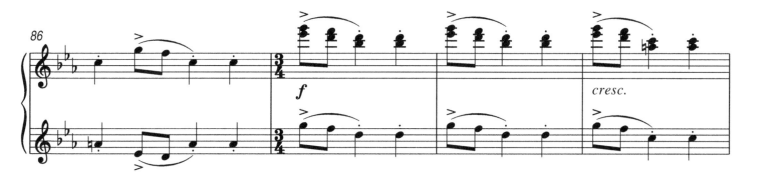

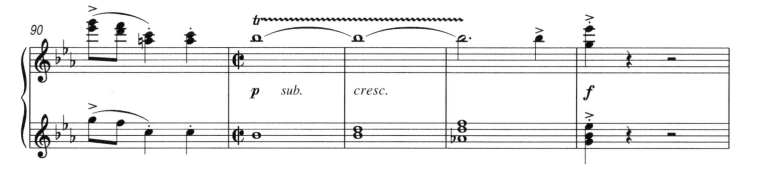

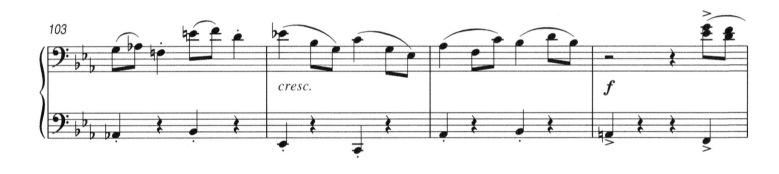

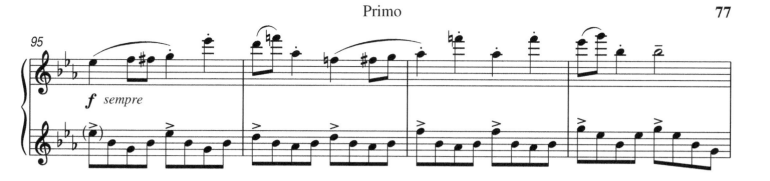

Secondo

We Are Women
(Polka)

Allegretto con grazia

Leonard Bernstein
Arranged by C Harmon

We Are Women
(Polka)

Allegretto con grazia

Leonard Bernstein
Arranged by C Harmon

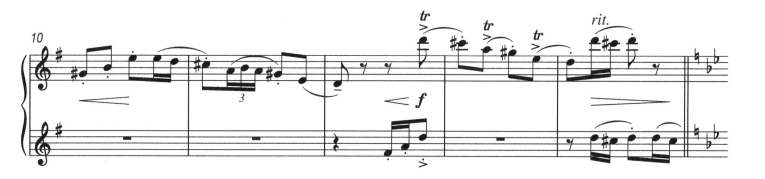

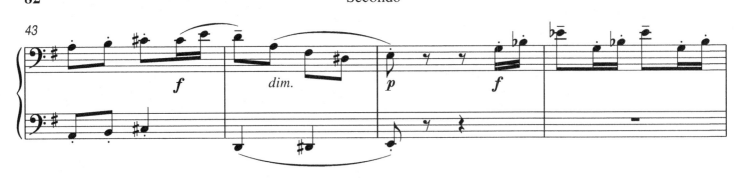

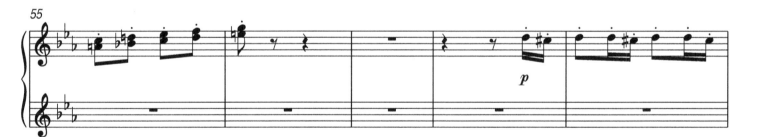

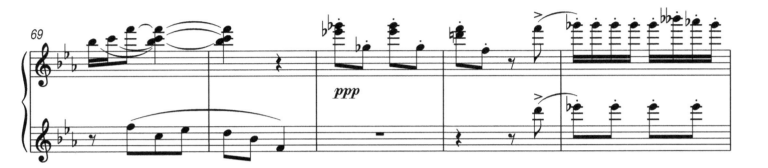

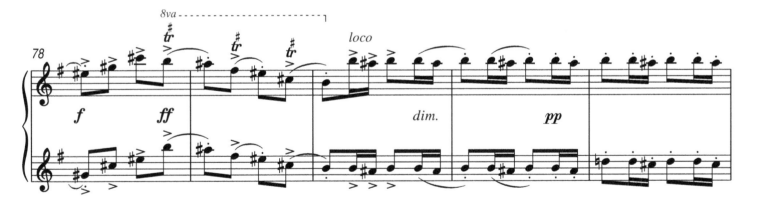

87

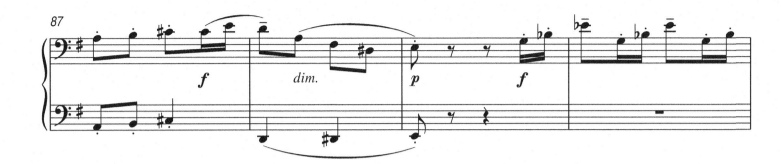

91

quasi cadenza

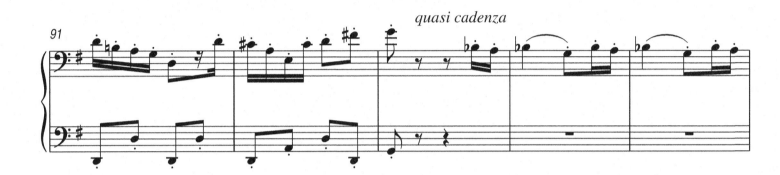

96

Presto

101

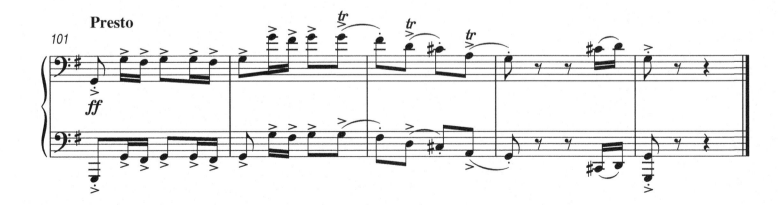

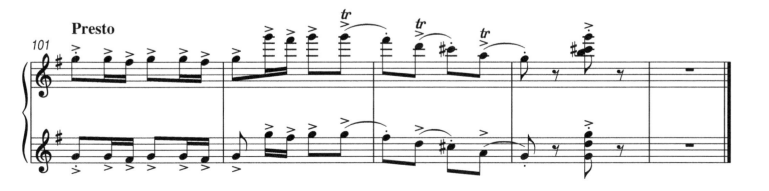

Make Our Garden Grow

Andante moderato

Leonard Bernstein
Arranged by C Harmon

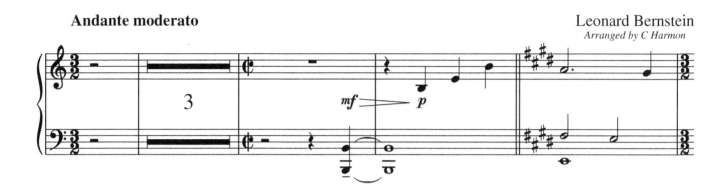

Make Our Garden Grow

Andante moderato

Leonard Bernstein
Arranged by C Harmon

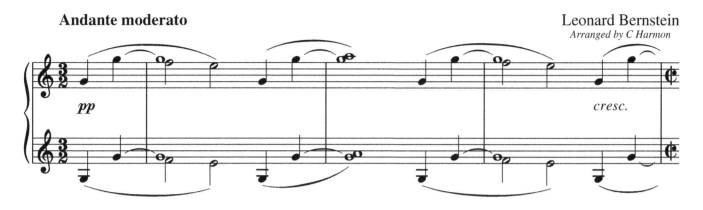

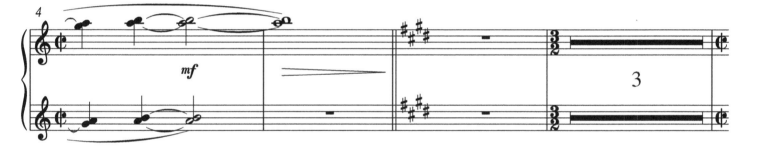

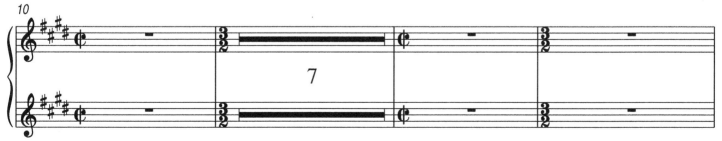

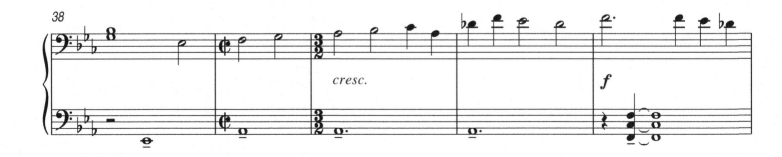

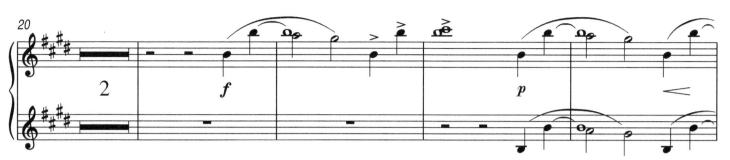

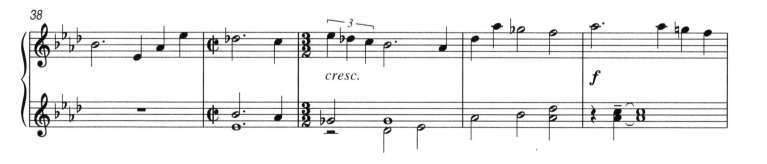

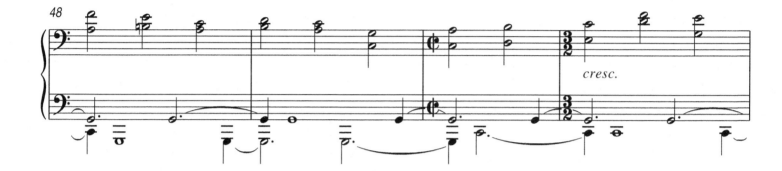

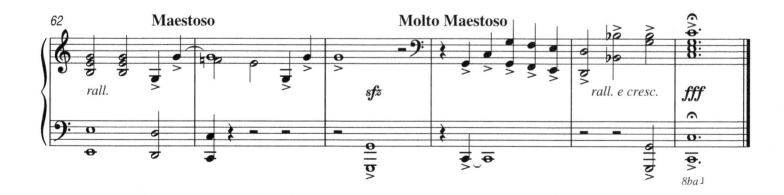

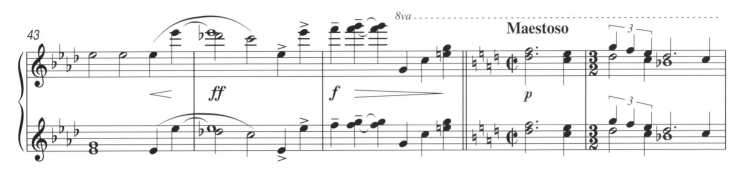

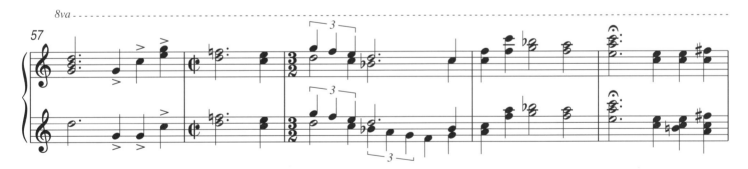